Two Becoming One, God's Plan

By
Lonzo Bullock and Lyn Bullock

BP

bullock
publishing

Contents

Copyright

COPYRIGHT

Dedication

This book is dedicated to our village that supports us through thick and thin as well as the village that made us—Brick City & Park Hill.

[24] That is why a man leaves his father and mother and is united to his wife, and they become one flesh.

Genesis 2:24, NIV Bible

Introduction

This book is written from our perspective as a newly married couple. We do not profess to have all the answers, but we know that we are trying to learn to love each other every day. We didn't have anyone to share love gems with us, so we want to make sure to leave a legacy of love with this book.

Preparing for a marriage based in faith first involves accepting our Creator as your guide. Marriage requires joint prayer, faith, and belief in our Creator. A great marriage comes from Him! Your main focus should be your relationship with God. You may not always be consistent and perfect, but you should aim to follow God's path. God will not lead us astray, and a clear path is vital for preparing for marriage.

We must learn to understand the reason for giving our life to God. God provides peace, blessings, and understanding. As life becomes complicated, God can sustain us to not sway based on what we see. A man must uphold himself and his family. It is difficult to steady yourself during a storm. But if you also have to steady and lead a family during tumultuous times, you need confidence in your decisions. God brings self-assurance, healing, and protection that allow a husband to provide those same attributes to his family.

We recommend that this book be reviewed as a couple, and the exercises shared together. This book is meant to be an interactive guide so that it's possible to make an informed step in the next phase of your life.

Chapter 1

Do You Have Common Goals?

Meditation: 2 Corinthians 6:14–18 (NIV)

¹⁴ Do not be yoked together with unbelievers. For what do righteousness and wickedness have in common? Or what fellowship can light have with darkness? ¹⁵ What harmony is there between Christ and Belial? Or what does a believer have in common with an unbeliever? ¹⁶ What agreement is there between the temple of God and Idols? For we are the temple of the living God. As God has said:

"I will live with them

and walk among them,

and I will be their God,

and they will be my people."

¹⁷ Therefore,

"Come out from them

and be separate,"

says the Lord.

"Touch no unclean thing,

  and I will receive you."

[18] And,

"I will be a Father to you,

  and you will be my sons and daughters,"

says the Lord Almighty.

Prayer

Heavenly Father, I pray that you reveal our heart's intentions toward you. Please guide our focus to surround ourselves with those who are equally yoked with us. Please guide our steps to grow together as we yield to you. In Jesus' name, I pray. Amen.

His Perspective

We must have purposeful relationships in all facets of our life, but especially in marriage. Prepare your marriage for a positive outcome by asking God for wisdom and meaning in your union. God will give you, as a couple, the wisdom to use each other's differences to build a unit that is equally yoked, sustainable, and formidable.

As you prepare for marriage, share your feelings and thoughts with an open mind to find meaningful ways to build a strong bond. If you are both willing to allow God to release His power in you, God will intertwine with your union.

God is love and values love. For love to be the center of your marriage, God must be your central focus. Being focused and patient for God's Will to be done protects and covers the marriage. Two people equally focused on God leads to a fruitful marriage.

Her Perspective

Dating is an opportunity to learn another person's mind and soul. You will never know everything about a person. Still, dating should have given you an opportunity to assess the person's overall habits. Lifestyle and behaviors indicate a person's propensity for success in any area of their life.

You can't expect to have a strong relationship with God if you never pray, attend church, perform worship and praise, be of service, or give to others. Your willingness to give time to God and sacrifice some of your life reflects the importance of your spiritual life. You will know from the dating process if the person you are seeing has habits that are equally yoked with your habits. If you are with a mate who refuses to go to church with you because they want to watch a football game or their favorite TV show, then there may be a conflict.

I do not recommend immediately ending the relationship. But it could help to have a discussion with the person about the importance of their spiritual life. Suppose there is an ongoing issue with your agreement about spiritual life. In that case, you might reconsider if this person is meant to be a friend or a partner for life.

God will not bring you someone who pulls you from Him. God will bless you with a mate who guides you closer to His Will for your life.

Exercise

Reflect and meditate on how the person brings you closer to God in each spiritual area below.

a. How does my partner help me improve my prayer life?

b. How do we encourage each other to be of service?

c. Are we on the same page with donating time and money to the church?

d. Are we both active in the church? Is being active important to me?

e. What faith do I want to practice?

f. Do you believe God is the head of your household?

After discussing your answers with your partner, identify areas of your spiritual life that are not in sync. You don't have to solve the issues now. The purpose is to be aware of how you both feel about and approach your spiritual life.

Notes:

Chapter 2

What Is Your Purpose for Marriage?

Meditation: Ecclesiastes 4:7–12 (NIV)

[7] Again I saw something meaningless under the sun:

[8] There was a man all alone;

he had neither son nor brother.

There was no end to his toil,

yet his eyes were not content with his wealth.

"For whom am I toiling," he asked,

"and why am I depriving myself of enjoyment?"

This too is meaningless—

a miserable business!

[9] Two are better than one,

because they have a good return for their labor:

[10] If either of them falls down,

one can help the other up.

But pity anyone who falls

and has no one to help them up.

[11] Also, if two lie down together, they will keep warm.

But how can one keep warm alone?

¹² Though one may be overpowered,

two can defend themselves.

A cord of three strands is not quickly broken.

Prayer

Heavenly Father, please guide me to understand our purpose for marriage. Please help us understand that marriage is the uniting of two in covenant with You. In Jesus' name, I pray. Amen.

His Perspective

Marriage is a physical manifestation of God's love for us. God made us for the purpose of loving each other and seeking companionship. We must not allow worldly lust and desires to distract us from the meaning of our marriage. Preparing for marriage requires prayerfully requesting God's meaning of marriage. God delivers clear and direct answers based on His Word.

God's love and wisdom for us will never put us in harm's way. God will move us toward a partner who shows His light. God wants a marriage to elevate our prayer and worship for Him. A relationship centered around selfishness and anger is not an honor to God. God is honored by two imperfect people who humbly and peacefully come together to worship Christ's perfect love for us.

Her Perspective

The statement that a cord of three strands can't be quickly broken is powerful in understanding the meaning of Christian marriage. Marriage is not simply the uniting of two souls. A biblical marriage brings two people in a relationship with God as the center of their union. The three-strand cord can hold more stress than you can hold as one person.

Marriage is designed to strengthen your bond with God as well as offer you a physical being whom you can lean on for strength when you are weak. The tying of the cords is symbolic of the strength and power that you will give and receive from each other. Marriage is not about one person solely holding up another person. The two of you should be intertwined. There will be times when the husband is the stronger cord and times when the wife is the stronger cord. The bond held together sustains the cords without any one cord being stronger.

You have to be in agreement about your purpose for marriage and belief in marriage. You must also know what you want out of the marriage. You will know if someone is a suitable match based on how you view marriage.

Exercise

What are your intentions for marriage? This exercise will help you to define your marriage mission and vision.

- What three words describe my reason for wanting to be married?
- Who is my role model for marriage?
- How do I expect marriage to serve God's Kingdom?
- Have I put more time into thinking about my ideal marriage than I put into thinking about my ideal wedding?
- What will be God's role in our marriage?
- What are my weaknesses that my potential mate strengthens?

- How do you define your marriage mission and vision?

By answering these questions, you will have a better understanding of the reasons you are contemplating getting married. This couple assessment is to ensure that you know what marriage means to you. Be honest with each other so that you can build a solid foundation.

After answering the questions, write out your dating mission vision using the template below.

We, (insert names), want a marriage that resembles (insert your role model). We want the relationship to have (each list your three characteristics from the first bullet). We plan to serve God's Kingdom (list out the items from the third bullet). Our union will build a three-cord string by complementing each other (list out the last bullet items).

As you consider marriage, pray as a unit over your mission and vision to receive guidance from God. Notes:

Chapter 3

Do You Both Value Family?

Meditation: 1 John 4:7–12 (NIV)

7 Dear friends, let us love one another, for love comes from God. Everyone who loves has been born of God and knows God. 8 Whoever does not love does not know God, because God is love. 9 This is how God showed his love among us: He sent his one and only Son into the world that we might live through him. 10 This is love: not that we loved God, but that he loved us and sent his Son as an atoning sacrifice for our sins. 11 Dear friends, since God so loved us, we also ought to love one another. 12 No one has ever seen God; but if we love one another, God lives in us and his love is made complete in us.

Prayer

Heavenly Father, please teach us how to love each other as well as each other's family. We know that our love for others is a reflection of You. Please allow our love to be manifested and exemplified by how we treat our family with love, grace, and mercy. In Jesus' name, I pray. Amen.

His Perspective

Marriage is the unification of two value systems into one. The negotiation of the family value dynamics is the foundation for how the husband and wife make decisions about caring for parents and children throughout their lifetime. Suppose one of the parties in the union does not feel comfortable with the unified family values; in that case, there will always be tension in the marriage.

It is important to share family values with your spouse. My wife is the most loving and caring woman a man could have in his life. I am thankful to God for my wife. She loves family immensely and is willing to make sacrifices. When dating my wife, I saw her love for family through her actions. Our common understanding of the importance of family has been a blessing as we support each other to integrate our families.

As you raise children and support aging parents, it is a blessing to have a partner who loves your family as their own. When preparing for marriage, cultivate values that can sustain your maturing family for a lifetime.

Her Perspective

I never considered the importance of melding two families together until I got married. My husband's love for my mother has made me fall more in love with him. He immediately opened his heart to treat my mother as he would treat his mother. It's evident that he loves my mother because he views her as an extension of me.

My husband has always valued family connections. His character is centered around God and family. Being with someone who always has valued family makes it easier to navigate issues that arise with our families. My husband's willingness to treat my mother as if she were his mother removes the stress of trying to make everyone get along.

Our unit naturally included our parents because we genuinely value our parents and are in agreement on how to love them. Just as my husband loves my mother, I adore his mother. I immensely appreciate her for raising a great man who loves everyone around him.

Exercise

You and your partner should discuss the importance of family in your life. The questions below should be discussed. Allow each person to express their feelings without any judgment or interruption. Simply listen to each other and gather responses. Then review each question to find common ground.

Question	Partner Response	Partner Response	Comments
How often do you see your immediate family?			
What is your belief on taking care of elderly parents?			
How do you envision splitting time between			

Question	Partner Response	Partner Response	Comments
families for holidays?			
Do you believe that you need to assist your parents financially?			
If you are coming into the relationship with kids, you should discuss what you see as your parenting role.			
Do your families share the same religion? If not, how will you respect each family's beliefs?			

Notes:

Chapter 4

Do You Have the Same Beliefs About Money?

Meditation: Matthew 25:14–30 (NIV)

14 "Again, it will be like a man going on a journey, who called his servants and entrusted his wealth to them. 15 To one he gave five bags of gold, to another two bags, and to another one bag, each according to his ability. Then he went on his journey. 16 The man who had received five bags of gold went at once and put his money to work and gained five bags more. 17 So also, the one with two bags of gold gained two more. 18 But the man who had received one bag went off, dug a hole in the ground and hid his master's money.

19 "After a long time the master of those servants returned and settled accounts with them. 20 The man who had received five bags of gold brought the other

five. 'Master,' he said, 'you entrusted me with five bags of gold. See, I have gained five more.'

21 "His master replied, 'Well done, good and faithful servant! You have been faithful with a few things; I will put you in charge of many things. Come and share your master's happiness!'

22 "The man with two bags of gold also came. 'Master,' he said, 'you entrusted me with two bags of gold; see, I have gained two more.'

23 "His master replied, 'Well done, good and faithful servant! You have been faithful with a few things; I will put you in charge of many things. Come and share your master's happiness!'

24 "Then the man who had received one bag of gold came. 'Master,' he said, 'I knew that you are a hard man, harvesting where you have not sown and gathering where you have not scattered seed. 25 So I

was afraid and went out and hid your gold in the ground. See, here is what belongs to you.'

²⁶ "His master replied, 'You wicked, lazy servant! So, you knew that I harvest where I have not sown and gather where I have not scattered seed? ²⁷ Well then, you should have put my money on deposit with the bankers, so that when I returned, I would have received it back with interest.

²⁸ "'So take the bag of gold from him and give it to the one who has ten bags. ²⁹ For whoever has will be given more, and they will have an abundance. Whoever does not have, even what they have will be taken from them. ³⁰ And throw that worthless servant outside, into the darkness, where there will be weeping and gnashing of teeth.'

Prayer

Dear Lord, thank You for the resources that You have provided us. Please teach us to be on one accord with using our resources to glorify Your Kingdom. In Jesus' name, I pray. Amen.

His Perspective

Money can be a difficult subject in marriage since we are raised having different relationships with money. Some people are raised to save money to express their value, and some people are raised to spend money on luxury items to express their value. Both may want to be considered worthy, but they both may use money differently to prove their value. Our different money mindsets make it difficult to become one without reaching common ground.

Finding common ground will challenge us to each address our emotional feelings about money.

Money is currency, and currency is energy, and energy can be good or bad vibrations. The emotion around money will determine if you sow good or bad seeds for the future. You don't want to plant seeds that you intend to use for a future harvest, and as soon as you plant the seeds, your spouse is pulling them up. You will never have any harvest in life if you don't share the same plan for your collective energy.

Our grandparents married early in life without anything, so they were able to build a common current framework. Many of us are marrying later in life when we have already built our individual currency framework. As you prepare to build with your spouse, focus on the long-term prize and how you can collectively develop a legacy for your family, which also includes God's Will.

Her Perspective

The relationship with money can be a source of contention within your life as a married or single person. A healthy relationship with money requires balance. You should be able to spend as well as save.

If you are someone who saves 70 percent of their salary, it will be difficult to marry someone who only saves 20 percent of their income. The person who spends more money may feel constrained and judged by the other person's requirements to save and delay gratification.

The person who likes to save may feel stressed by the other person's spending habits. Coming together requires negotiating a balance with each person's needs being considered. You both may have to give in order to find peace within your relationship with money and each other.

Exercise

Understanding each person's relationship with money requires honest and difficult communication. The questions below are icebreakers to assist with finding a balance between how you spend and save money.

1. Using the chart below, detail how you each spend money using the percentage of your monthly income.

Budget Categories	Partner	Partner
Rent/Mortgage/Utilities		
Auto/Transportation		
Healthcare including Insurance		
Education/Reinvestment in Yourself		
Travel/Concerts/Leisure		
Church and Charity		
Savings		
Retirement		
Credit Cards		
Student Loans		
Shopping		
Child Care		
Food		
Insurance premiums (long-term, life, accidental)		

2. As you review each person's spending profile, you should have an honest conversation about how you feel about the amount you are each saving and spending. Below defines a plan that you each feel comfortable with if you are in the same household.

Budget Categories	Our Planned Spending Profile
Rent/Mortgage/Utilities	
Auto/Transportation	
Healthcare including Insurance	
Education/Reinvestment in Yourself	
Travel/Concerts/Leisure	
Church and Charity	
Savings	
Retirement	
Credit Cards	
Student Loans	
Shopping	
Child Care	
Food	
Insurance premiums (long-term, life, accidental)	

In addition to the spending profile, you should ask each other the following questions:

- Do you have any bankruptcies, foreclosures, or liens/judgments?
- What is your credit score?
- At what age do you want to retire?
- Do you have life, disability, and/or long-term care insurance coverage?
- What are your career goals?
- Do you plan to work if we have a family?

Notes:

Chapter 5

Are You Both Accountable?

Meditation: Matthew 7:3–5 (NIV)

3 "Why do you look at the speck of sawdust in your brother's eye and pay no attention to the plank in your own eye? 4 How can you say to your brother, 'Let me take the speck out of your eye,' when all the time there is a plank in your own eye? 5 You hypocrite, first take the plank out of your own eye, and then you will see clearly to remove the speck from your brother's eye."

Prayer

Heavenly Father, please teach me to be accountable for my actions. Please allow me to honor the truth of my actions and to correct myself to be aligned with Your will. In Jesus' name, I pray. Amen.

His Perspective

A great marriage requires nonjudgmental accountability. A spiritually healthy couple will carry each other's burdens when the other person is weak while jointly taking ownership for good and bad actions. When a spouse has success, the couple jointly celebrates and takes pride in the success. When one falls, both should be accountable. Sustain each other's shortcomings with love and not condemnation.

Seeing your spouse's actions as your own will allow you to be more compassionate. God sees how we treat the person we vow to honor in front of Him. As you take your vows, remember that you are making a promise to love each other, allowing God to be the only judge.

Her Perspective

It is easy to criticize others, and it is difficult to review your own actions. I have found myself quick to identify how someone else has done me wrong. But it takes more time to find out how I have done someone else wrong. Emotional maturity will result in your being willing to review yourself before you criticize someone else.

A successful marriage requires accountability. You have to be willing to work on your faults as much as you identify your spouse's faults. It is difficult to date someone who refuses to be accountable for their actions.

If the person you are dating doesn't know how to be accountable, you will feel like you are dating a perpetual child. You both have to be willing to grow and move toward your best.

Exercise

For the exercise below, you and your partner should each write what you want to improve in each area of your life. Have an honest conversation about what you think you should improve about yourself.

	Partner 1	Partner 2
How would you improve your spiritual life?		
How would you improve your health?		
How would you improve your financial well-being?		
How would you improve your family relationships?		

Notes:

Chapter 6

Are You Emotionally Supportive Of Each Other?

Meditation: Ephesians 4:2–3 (NIV)

2 Be completely humble and gentle; be patient, bearing with one another in love. 3 Make every effort to keep the unity of the Spirit through the bond of peace.

Prayer

Heavenly Father, please teach us to become emotionally supportive of each other. Allow us to be emotionally supportive of each other by being humble, gentle, patient, and kind. In Jesus' name, I pray. Amen.

His Perspective

Never underestimate the importance of having a supportive partner. There are times when life can be difficult, and you need a cheerleader and helpmate. God expects us to be humble and patient with our spouse even when we don't feel like it. Supporting the other person is more than just listening. Being supportive is a gift to your spouse that builds a bond of peace.

Her Perspective

Learning to be emotionally supportive is required for a loving relationship. You and your partner deserve someone who will lift you up when you are down, as well as celebrate your successes. The person who God has for you will mimic God's love for you.

You want to marry someone who is loving, kind, humble, and patient. Search your heart to make sure you treat your mate with the dignity and respect God gives you. If you are not striving to treat your mate the way God treats you, you may not be ready to be a spouse and vice versa. God is not going to bring us someone who is not aligned with His Will for us to be loved and supported.

Exercise

Describe how each of you provides support for the other using the words listed below.

	Partner 1	Partner 2
Patient—How do I display patience in our relationship?		
Humble—How do I show that I am humble?		
Love—How am I loving?		
Unity—How does our relationship reflect unity?		
Peace—How do I bring peace to my partner?		
Gentle—How am I gentle?		

Notes:

Chapter 7

Are You Able to Forgive Each Other?

Meditation: Ephesians 4:25–32 (NIV)

25 Therefore each of you must put off falsehood and speak truthfully to your neighbor, for we are all members of one body. **26** "In your anger do not sin": Do not let the sun go down while you are still angry, **27** and do not give the devil a foothold. **28** Anyone who has been stealing must steal no longer, but must work, doing something useful with their own hands, that they may have something to share with those in need.

29 Do not let any unwholesome talk come out of your mouths, but only what is helpful for building others up according to their needs, that it may benefit those who listen. **30** And do not grieve the Holy Spirit of God, with whom you were sealed for the day of redemption. **31**

Get rid of all bitterness, rage and anger, brawling and slander, along with every form of malice. [32] Be kind and compassionate to one another, forgiving each other, just as in Christ God forgave you.

Prayer

Heavenly Father, please teach me not to hold any malice or anger toward others. Please allow me to be a vessel of forgiveness. In Jesus' name, I pray. Amen.

His Perspective

A foundational principle of the Bible is that we must forgive others as quickly as we want God to forgive us. Do not hold on to your spouse's wrongdoings. A husband and wife must be quicker to forgive each other than to get angry with each other. Disagreements and disappointments fertilize a relationship in preparation for God's blessings. Take the lessons from the disappointments, but do not live in the negative experiences. Create an atmosphere of forgiveness in your household, and God will bless your household to be forgiven. Your marriage is love; God is love, and He forgives us every day when we fall short of His expectations. Give your spouse the same love that God has given us.

Her Perspective

Anger can impact you physically, spiritually, and mentally. Anger is toxic and doesn't manifest positive growth. If you want to spend a lifetime with someone, you have to be able to build a relationship based on effective communication and forgiveness. You must build your relationship on the willingness to forgive each other. You have to be two people who look for the best in each other.

Exercise

List how you each deal with anger and forgiveness.

	Partner 1	Partner 2
How do you process anger? Do you talk to others? Pray? Sleep?		
What do you dislike about how the other person manages anger?		

Notes:

Chapter 8

Do You Sharpen Each Other?

Meditation: Proverbs 27:17 (NIV)

[17] As iron sharpens iron,

so one person sharpens another.

Prayer

Heavenly Father, I pray that You confirm that we are equally yoked and sharpen each other. Please surround me with people who bring out the best in me. In Jesus' name, I pray. Amen.

His Perspective

God sends you a mate who can help you grow closer to Him. In the Bible, Matthew 18:20 states that God is present where there are two or more gathered in His name. Two Christians are made of the same material so that they can sharpen each other. The sharpening comes through jointly praying in His name and interceding on behalf of each other. Over time, you teach each other spiritually, which elevates your love beyond anything physical in this world.

Her Perspective

Iron sharpens iron because it is made from the same material. Iron can't sharpen cotton because iron and cotton are two different materials. It's best to pair yourself with someone who is made from the same material as you and be equally yoked. Also, the person must be able to bring out the best in you.

When you marry someone, you become one. You want to become one with someone who exemplifies the characteristics that you value. You also want to be with someone who can make you grow in new ways and add value to your character. While you date someone, take note of how they make you better and how you make them better.

Exercise

Take inventory of the ways you make each other better.

	Partner 1	Partner 2
How does my partner make me better spiritually?		
How do I make my partner better spiritually?		
How does my partner make me better as a family member?		
How do I make my partner better as a family member?		
How does my partner make me be a better person with my life goals?		
How do I make my partner better at achieving their life goals?		

Notes:

Chapter 9

How Do You Communicate?

Meditation: Colossians 4:2–6 (NIV)

4 ² Devote yourselves to prayer, being watchful and thankful. ³ And pray for us, too, that God may open a door for our message, so that we may proclaim the mystery of Christ, for which I am in chains. ⁴ Pray that I may proclaim it clearly, as I should. ⁵ Be wise in the way you act toward outsiders; make the most of every opportunity. ⁶ Let your conversation be always full of grace, seasoned with salt, so that you may know how to answer everyone.

Prayer

Heavenly Father, please teach me to communicate with grace. Please let my words edify others and produce fruit that reflects You. In Jesus' name, I pray. Amen.

His Perspective

Communicate to your spouse like Jesus communicated to the Church. Your words with your spouse should edify and protect. Words are like pictures that can never be removed from someone's mind. You don't want your communication footprint to leave your mate with bad memories. Your goal should be to leave your spouse with the best of you.

Her Perspective

It took me years to understand how my words manifest into actions. My words can change the energy when I am speaking to someone, especially my husband. I know what to say to calm a disagreement or add to it. I purposely choose my words to encourage my husband and to remove any negativity.

My goal is not to be right or to prove myself superior to my husband. We are one, so there is no benefit in bringing the other person down. I benefit from having my husband feel uplifted when he communicates with me. I pray daily for God to bring me the words that will encourage and heal my husband. Even when we disagree, I try to take a moment to make sure that my point is expressed in love.

Exercise

You and your partner should spend some time discussing with each other what you like and don't like about your current communication style.

	Partner 1	Partner 2
What triggers you about my communication style?		
What do you like about my communication style?		
Do you prefer having serious discussions in the morning or night?		

Notes:

Chapter 10

Does Your Relationship Yield the Fruits of The Spirit?

Meditation: Galatians 5:13–26 (NIV)

¹³ You, my brothers and sisters, were called to be free. But do not use your freedom to indulge the flesh; rather, serve one another humbly in love. ¹⁴ For the entire law is fulfilled in keeping this one command: "Love your neighbor as yourself." ¹⁵ If you bite and devour each other, watch out or you will be destroyed by each other.

¹⁶ So I say, walk by the Spirit, and you will not gratify the desires of the flesh. ¹⁷ For the flesh desires what is contrary to the Spirit, and the Spirit what is contrary to the flesh. They are in conflict with each other, so that you are not to do whatever you want. ¹⁸ But if you are led by the Spirit, you are not under the law.

[19] The acts of the flesh are obvious: sexual immorality, impurity and debauchery; [20] idolatry and witchcraft; hatred, discord, jealousy, fits of rage, selfish ambition, dissensions, factions [21] and envy; drunkenness, orgies, and the like. I warn you, as I did before, that those who live like this will not inherit the kingdom of God.

[22] But the fruit of the Spirit is love, joy, peace, forbearance, kindness, goodness, faithfulness, [23] gentleness and self-control. Against such things there is no law. [24] Those who belong to Christ Jesus have crucified the flesh with its passions and desires. [25] Since we live by the Spirit, let us keep in step with the Spirit. [26] Let us not become conceited, provoking and envying each other.

Prayer

Heavenly Father, please guide me to allow our life to reflect the fruit of the Spirit. In Jesus' name, we pray. Amen.

His Perspective

Love is the center of a healthy marriage. When you are ready to take your vows, you are committing to leaving your former self. You two become the "new you." The "new you" are jointly one under Him. Your fleshly desires should be buried in exchange for spiritual fruit. A life of spiritual fruit is your reward for putting God's Will first in your marriage.

Her Perspective

Conduct yourself in love and strive to demonstrate the fruit of the Spirit. No one is perfect, but you should strive to show love, joy, peace, forbearance, kindness, goodness, faithfulness, [23] gentleness, and self-control.

Exercise

Answer the questions below.

- How do we reflect the fruit of the Spirit as a couple?

- How does our relationship reflect love?

- How does our relationship reflect joy?

- How does our relationship reflect peace?

- How does our relationship reflect forbearance?

- How does our relationship reflect kindness?

- How does our relationship reflect goodness?

- How does our relationship reflect faithfulness?

- How does our relationship reflect gentleness?

- How does our relationship reflect self-control?

Notes:

Chapter 11

Reflections

As you consider spending your life with someone, consider all the key points of this book. Be open to discussing them and be honest with each other. We also want you to seek wise counsel. Do not rely on your own understanding before deciding to make a commitment. Marriage is life-changing, and you are connecting your life to a person. Connecting your life to someone can determine your entire future.

Proverbs 12 (NIV)

12 Whoever loves discipline loves knowledge,

but whoever hates correction is stupid.

[2] Good people obtain favor from the LORD,

but he condemns those who devise wicked

schemes.

³ No one can be established through wickedness,

but the righteous cannot be uprooted.

⁴ A wife of noble character is her husband's crown,

but a disgraceful wife is like decay in his bones.

⁵ The plans of the righteous are just,

but the advice of the wicked is deceitful.

⁶ The words of the wicked lie in wait for blood,

but the speech of the upright rescues them.

⁷ The wicked are overthrown and are no more,

but the house of the righteous stands firm.

⁸ A person is praised according to their prudence,

and one with a warped mind is despised.

⁹ Better to be a nobody and yet have a servant

than pretend to be somebody and have no food.

¹⁰ The righteous care for the needs of their animals,

but the kindest acts of the wicked are cruel.

¹¹ Those who work their land will have abundant food,

   but those who chase fantasies have no sense.

¹² The wicked desire the stronghold of evildoers,

   but the root of the righteous endures.

¹³ Evildoers are trapped by their sinful talk,

   and so the innocent escape trouble.

¹⁴ From the fruit of their lips people are filled with good

things, and the work of their hands brings them

reward.

¹⁵ The way of fools seems right to them,

   but the wise listen to advice.

¹⁶ Fools show their annoyance at once,

   but the prudent overlook an insult.

¹⁷ An honest witness tells the truth,

   but a false witness tells lies.

¹⁸ The words of the reckless pierce like swords,

   but the tongue of the wise brings healing.

[19] Truthful lips endure forever,

but a lying tongue lasts only a moment.

[20] Deceit is in the hearts of those who plot evil,

but those who promote peace have joy.

[21] No harm overtakes the righteous,

but the wicked have their fill of trouble.

[22] The LORD detests lying lips,

but he delights in people who are trustworthy.

[23] The prudent keep their knowledge to themselves,

but a fool's heart blurts out folly.

[24] Diligent hands will rule,

but laziness ends in forced labor.

[25] Anxiety weighs down the heart,

but a kind word cheers it up.

[26] The righteous choose their friends carefully,

but the way of the wicked leads them astray.

27 The lazy do not roast any game,

but the diligent feed on the riches of the hunt.

28 In the way of righteousness there is life;

along that path is immortality.

Prayers & Blessings

We've enjoyed sharing our experiences of using biblical principles to endure a long-distance marriage.

We hope you have seen how the book reflects on the way God can keep a couple strong, no matter the distance or circumstance. Through faith, prayer, praise, fasting, communication, setting priorities and goals, self-discipline, self-love, patience, loyalty, and giving, our marriage has been blessed. We recognize that God is in control at all times on our journey.

The next several pages are for journaling, for you and your spouse to write your thoughts on each principle.

With love,

Lonzo & Lyn

Journal

This section is for you and your spouse to write your thoughts on each principle to enhance your marriage.

1. Common Goals

2. Purpose for Marriage

3. Valuing Family

4. Beliefs

5. Accountability

6. Emotionally Supportive

7. Forgiving Each Other

8. Sharpening Each Other

9. Communication

10.   Fruits of The Spirit

11. Reflections

Books By this Author

DATING WITH A PURPOSE

https://www.amazon.com/dp/B08STV2P8L

This book highlights lessons learned from the authors who finally found love after surrendering their dating life to God. Dating with A Purpose, God's Plan walks you through the journey of two people who choose to commit their dating life to God. In the course of becoming closer to God, the couple built a foundation on Biblical principles for love and marriage.

DATING WITH A PURPOSE, GOD'S PLAN: THE 90 DAY JOURNAL

https://www.amazon.com/dp/B08T43V2L1

This is a 90-day journal to document goals and changes made to prepare you for marriage.

SURVIVING & THRIVING IN A LONG-DISTANCE MARRIAGE, GOD'S PLAN

https://www.amazon.com/dp/1736469207

This book reflects on how God can keep a couple strong no matter the distance or circumstance. Through faith, prayer, and praise, fasting, communication, setting priorities and goals, self-discipline, self-love, patience, loyalty, and giving, our marriage has been blessed. We recognize that God is in control at all times on our journey.

www.ingramcontent.com/pod-product-compliance
Lightning Source LLC
Chambersburg PA
CBHW071608040426
42452CB00008B/1278

www.ingramcontent.com/pod-product-compliance
Lightning Source LLC
Chambersburg PA
CBHW071608040426
42452CB00008B/1278